This book is dedicated to all of the mothers that advocate tirelessly for their children and to my Mom and Marie, both wonderful examples of unconditional love.

To Caleb
Thank you, my sweet snug bug, for reminding me that with love, perseverance and bravery, we can overcome any obstacle.

To Joshua
You've always been my sunshine, sweet Joshua. Your giving spirit and easy going nature have made my world a happier place.

To Stacy
Thank you for encouraging me to follow all my crazy dreams. Your support means everything and I will love you forever.

To my parents
Thank you for your unconditional love and for always believing in me. I love you.

Once upon a time, there was a little boy who was born into a very colorful world. As a child, he would reach out his little hand to collect as many colors as he could.

He borrowed a little **yellow** from the bright summer sun, **blue** from the clear sky, **green** from his Pop's lush grass and **purple** from his Nana's flower garden.

He snuck some **red** from a tiny ladybug, **orange** from the beautiful sunset and **pink** from the love radiating from his mother's heart.

Soon, it was time for the little boy to start school, so he gathered all his colors and set off for his first day.

The colorful boy loved to go to school. But as fall days turned to winter, and winter to spring, the little boy's colors began to fade.

He could not always understand what his teacher was explaining and he became frustrated. He kept hearing "He doesn't understand" and "He can't go on". One day, his colors completely faded away.

His mother saw her colorless little boy and exclaimed,

"Oh no, that just won't do! I will teach and comfort you."

All day long, the little boy's mother thought of how to fill her child with color again.

That night after he fell asleep, she went into his room and quietly opened his toy box. She slid open the hidden drawer and took out a gold and glittery magical key. It shone with the colors of the rainbow.

She took the key and tiptoed into the attic, where she kept an old, but very special trunk, given to her by her own mother.

Using the gold key, she opened the trunk and removed a magic wand and fairy wings.

The next morning, the mother woke her little boy by whispering **"I love you"** in his ear. She noticed the color **pink** coming back into his heart.

Later that day, while wearing her fairy wings, she picked up her magic wand and began to teach her little boy the letters of the alphabet, using all the tricks she knew. Very slowly, she began to see a little bit of **blue** from the sky coming back to him.

They continued to work together until it was time for the little boy to start first grade. They gathered up **pink** from his mother's love and **blue** from the clear sky and set off for school.

The little boy loved going to school. But, as the fall days turned to winter, and winter to spring, the little boy's colors began to fade. He could not understand how to count or add numbers together, so once again he became frustrated. He again heard " He doesn't understand" and "He can't go on." His mother saw her sad, colorless little boy and exclaimed,

"Oh no, that just won't do! I will teach and comfort you."

The mother once again put on her fairy wings, picked up her magic wand, and used all the tricks she could find to teach her little boy. Slowly, **pink** from her love and **yellow** from the bright summer sun came back to him. As he began to understand what his mother was teaching him, he could also see the beautiful color **blue** coming back.

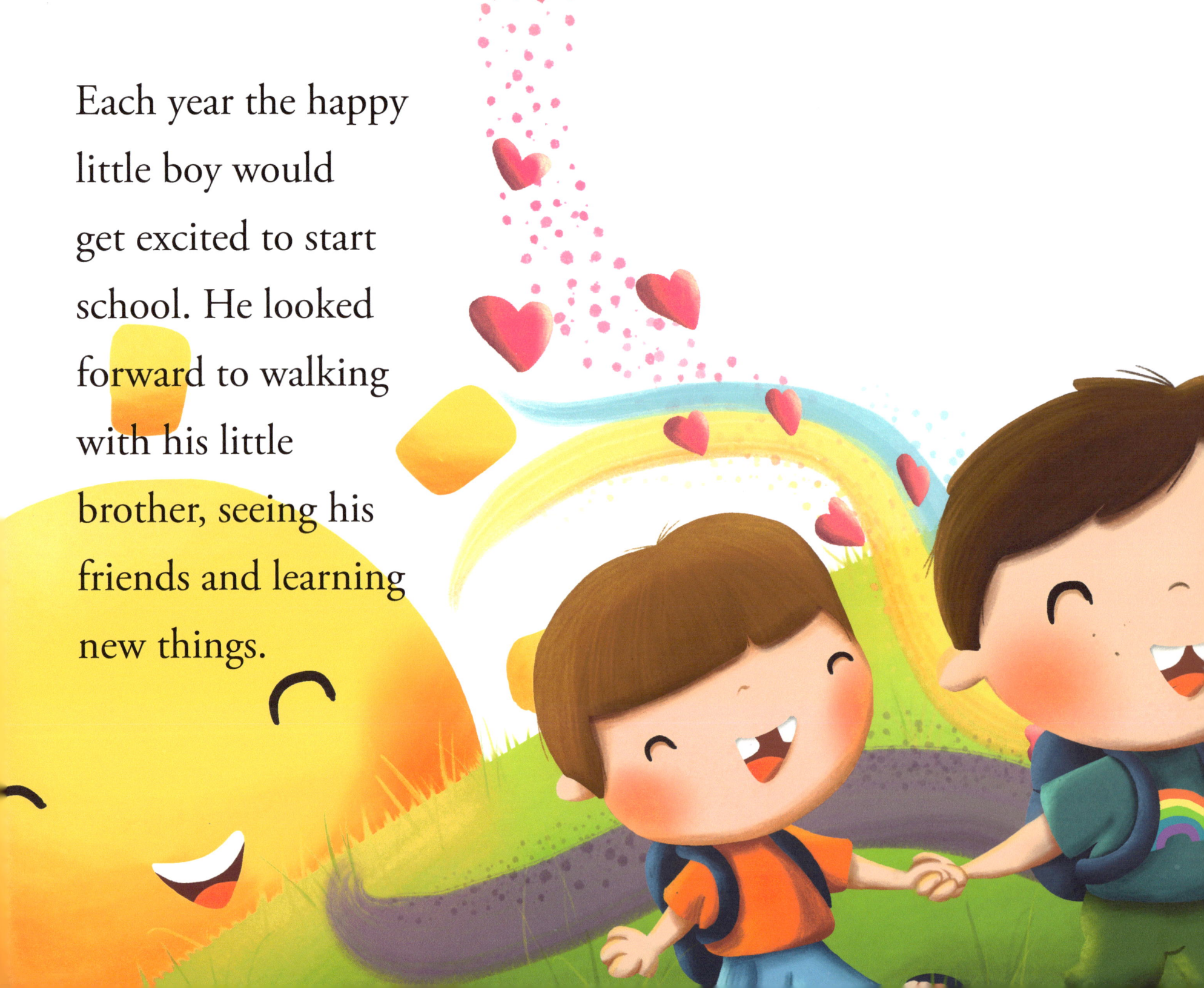

Each year the happy little boy would get excited to start school. He looked forward to walking with his little brother, seeing his friends and learning new things.

But, as the fall days turned to winter, and winter to spring, school again became harder and harder.

The once happy, colorful little boy became sadder and more frustrated as his colors grew lighter and lighter...

….so his mother put on her wings, pulled out her magic wand and used all her tricks to help her little boy learn what he did not understand.

The days turned to months, and the months turned to years, and the little boy became a young man.

Each year, as his mother put on her wings and used her magic wand, the young man would notice a new color reflecting back at him from his bedroom mirror.

Finally, he was filled with every color of the rainbow and his mother knew that it was time to put away her fairy wings and magic wand.

While the young man slept, she went into his room and quietly opened the secret drawer in his now forgotten toy box.

She took out the gold and glittery magical key that shone with the colors of the rainbow. Opening the special trunk that her mother had given her, she put away the fairy wings and magic wand.

As she took one last peek
into his room, she noticed
that it was filled with the colors
that would always be inside of him.

Pink was shining brightest of all
because it was the color that he collected
from the love radiating from her heart.

www.ingramcontent.com/pod-product-compliance
Lightning Source LLC
Chambersburg PA
CBHW041820080526

44589CB00004B/67